Watching Giraffes in Africa

Deborah Underwood

Heinemann Library
Chicago, Illinois

Customer Service   888-454-2279
Visit our website at www.heinemannlibrary.com

Designed by Ron Kamen and edesign
Illustrations by Martin Sanders
Printed and bound in China by South China Printing Company Limited

10 09 08 07 06
10 9 8 7 6 5 4 3 2 1

Library of Congress Cataloging-in-Publication Data
Underwood, Deborah.
  Watching giraffes in Africa / Deborah Underwood.
     p. cm. -- (Wild world)
  Includes bibliographical references. ISBN 1-4034-7230-0 (hardback : alk. paper) -- ISBN 1-4034-7243-2 (pbk. : alk. paper)
  1. Giraffe--Africa--Juvenile literature. I. Title. II. Series: Wild world (Chicago, Ill.)
  QL737.U56U53 2006
  599.638--dc22
                            2005023642

Acknowledgments
The author and publisher are grateful to the following for permission to reproduce copyright material: Ardea pp. **5** (Geoff Trinder), **14** (C. Clem Haagner), **18** (C. Clem Haagner); Corbis pp. **8** (Carl Purcell), **11**, **16** (Nigel J. Dennis), **20**, **26**; FLPA pp. **9** (Minden Pictures), **12** (Mitsuaki Iwago), **17** (Frans Lanting/Minden Pictures), **23** (Frans Lanting/Minden Pictures); Glenda Kapsalis p. **19**; Nature Picture Library pp. **10** (Pete Oxford), **22** (Jeff Foott); NHPA pp. **4** (Martin Harvey), **27** (Rich Kirchner), **29** bottom; Oxford Scientific Films p. **21** (Stan Osolinski); Photographers Direct pp. **24**, **25**; RichardPSmith.com p. **28**; Steve Bloom p. **15**; Still Pictures pp. **7**, **13**.

Cover photograph of giraffes reproduced with permission of NHPA (Martin Harvey).

The publishers would like to thank Michael Bright of the BBC Natural History Unit for his assistance in the preparation of this book. Every effort has been made to contact copyright holders of any material reproduced in this book. Any omissions will be rectified in subsequent printings if notice is given to the publisher. The paper used to print this book comes from sustainable resources.

Some words are shown in bold, **like this**. You can find out what they mean by looking in the glossary.

Contents

Meet the Giraffes

This is Africa, home of giraffes. Giraffes are the tallest **mammals** in the world. To find a giraffe, look for a long neck, long legs, and spots.

▼ *Giraffes are tall enough to peek into a second story window.*

There are many kinds of giraffes. Some have light brown spots shaped like stars. Others are covered with dark brown patches.

▶▶ *Each type of giraffe has spots that are shaped differently.*

At Home in Africa

The **continent** of Africa has many different **landscapes**. There are **woodlands** and flat grassy places called **savannas**. The savannas are dotted with trees.

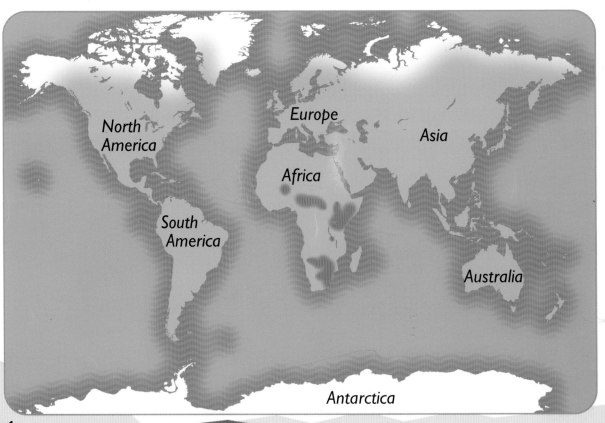

Key ● *This color shows where giraffes live in Africa.*

▲ *Giraffes share the savanna with zebras and other animals.*

The savannas are warm all year round. Rains soak the soil for many months each year. Green plants and grasses grow during this rainy season.

There's a Giraffe!

A giraffe's long legs and neck can look like tree trunks. They are sometimes hard to see because their spots help them blend in with the trees.

▲ *Giraffes are good at hiding, even though they are big.*

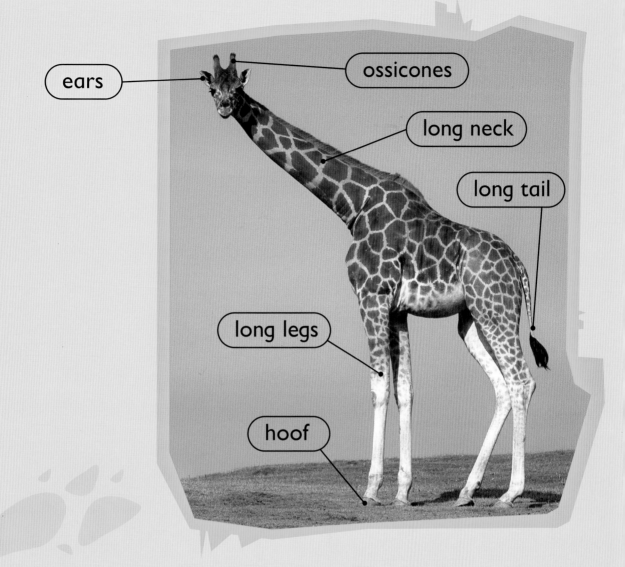

ears

ossicones

long neck

long tail

long legs

hoof

Giraffes have horn-like bumps called
ossicones on their heads. They flick away
flies with their long tails. Each **hoof** is the
size of a dinner plate.

Tasty Trees

The giraffes eat leaves, seeds, and pods from trees. Animals that eat leaves are called **browsers**. Giraffes like leaves from the **acacia** tree best.

▼ The acacia trees have very sharp spikes as well as tasty leaves.

There are very few other browsers that can reach these branches.

Giraffes need to eat a lot because they are so big. Their long necks let them pick food that most other animals can't reach.

How Giraffes Eat

A hungry giraffe grabs a branch with his long tongue. He pulls the branch into his mouth. Then he uses his teeth to scrape off the leaves.

*Giraffe's hairy lips protect them from the **acacia's** thorns.*

The giraffes swallow their food quickly. They do not chew it much at first. Later, the food travels back up into their mouths so they can chew it more.

▶▶ *Giraffes eat quickly, then chew their food later.*

On the Move

Walking giraffes move both feet on one side, then both feet on the other. This keeps their legs from getting tangled. Their necks bob up and down with each step.

Giraffes rock from side to side as they walk.

If they see a **predator**, the giraffes run away. Their long legs let them move quickly. They can **gallop** as fast as cars drive.

🔺 *Giraffes would rather run from danger than fight.*

The Dry Season

When the **savanna's** long dry season begins, green grasses turn brown. Plants dry out. The giraffes move closer to lakes and **water holes**. Green plants still grow there.

During the dry season giraffes look for water.

The giraffe must spread out its front legs or bend them to reach water.

The giraffe must lower its head to drink. With its head down, it is hard to watch for **predators**. Luckily, a giraffe can go for many days without drinking.

Giraffes Together

Giraffes move in a group called a **herd**. Some herds are large and some are small. Herds are always changing. The giraffes move from one group to another.

Herds can be made up of males, or **females** with children, or all three.

Giraffes are so tall that they can see **predators** from far away. They can spot danger long before it arrives.

🔺 *One or two of the giraffes stand watch while the others rest.*

Giraffe Babies

One of the **females** is ready to have a baby. She gives birth standing up. The baby enters the world with a thump as it falls to the ground!

▶▶ *A mother licks her new baby to clean it.*

Baby giraffes are as tall as an adult human.

Baby giraffes stand up before they are an hour old. They drink milk from their mother. They begin eating plants when they are one month old.

Growing Up

The baby and mother stay by themselves for a few weeks. This gives the baby a chance to get stronger. Then its mother takes it to meet the **herd**.

▼ *Baby giraffes can be born at any time of the year.*

▲ *This **female** giraffe watches the young giraffes while their mothers eat.*

The mother giraffes take turns caring for the herd's children. One mother watches many young giraffes. The other mothers go off to find food.

23

Under Attack

Leopards, lions, crocodiles, and **hyenas** may attack young giraffes. Lions are the only animals that may try to kill healthy adult giraffes.

▲ *Even lions have a hard time catching a giraffe.*

Giraffes can see a long way. Sneaking up on them is not easy. If a giraffe is attacked, it defends itself by kicking its strong front **hooves**.

▼ *A giraffe's powerful hoof can break the bones of a **predator**.*

Rainy Season

When the rains come, the **savannas** come alive with new growth. Brown grasses turn green. Soon new **acacia** leaves will sprout on the trees.

▼ *The rains mean new plants and more food for the giraffes.*

▲ *Young giraffes stay with their mothers for at least a year.*

Herds of giraffes spread out across the savanna. After the long dry season, giraffes will once again find tender new leaves to eat.

Tracker's Guide

When you want to watch animals in the wild, you need to find them first. You can look for clues they leave behind.

◀◀ *A giraffe's hoofprint is about the same size as a dinner plate.*

◀◀ As they move across the **savanna** looking for food, giraffes leave droppings behind. They look a bit like big acorns.

browse line

▶▶ Sometimes you can tell where giraffes have eaten. A browse line shows how far they have reached to eat.

Glossary

acacia thorny tree that grows on savannas

browser animal who eats leaves

continent the world is divided into seven large areas of land called continents. Each continent is divided into different countries.

female animal that can become a mother when it grows up. Women and girls are female people.

gallop to run quickly on four legs, like a horse

herd group of animals that live and travel together

hoof hard covering on the feet of some animals

hyena wolf-like animal that eats other animals

landscape type of land found in a place. A landscape can have mountains, rivers, forests, and many other things.

male animal that can become a father when it grows up. Men and boys are male people.

mammal animal that feeds its babies with the mother's milk

mate when male and female animals produce young. "Mate" can also mean the partner that an animal chooses to have babies with.

ossicone horn-like bump on a giraffe's head

predator animal that catches and eats other animals for food

savanna area of land mostly covered in sandy soil and grass with some trees and bushes

water hole pool where animals go to drink water

woodland land with many trees

Find Out More

Books

Foster, Leila. *Africa*. Chicago: Heinemann Library, 2001.

Ganeri, Anita. *Animal Life Cycles*. Chicago: Heinemann Library, 2005.

Kendell, Patricia. *Giraffes*. Chicago: Raintree, 2004.

An older reader can help you with these books:

Parker, Barbara Keevil. *Giraffes*. Minneapolis, Minn.: Carolrhoda Books, 2004.

Watt, E. Melanie. *Giraffes*. Austin, Tex.: Raintree Steck-Vaughn Publishers, 2002.

Wexo, John Bonnett. *Giraffes*. Poway, Calif.: Wildlife Education, Ltd., 2003.

Index